long a
and i with
final e

The First to Fly:
The True Story of the Wright Brothers

by Adrienne Betz
Illustrated by Marcy Dunn Ramsey

SCHOLASTIC INC.
v York Toronto London Auckland Sydney Mexico City New Delhi Hong Kong

Wilbur and Orville Wright were born more than one hundred years ago. When they were boys, there were no cars rumbling down the roads—there were just a few odd-looking bicycles. There were no airplanes streaking through the skies. Why not?

Cars, modern bikes, and airplanes had not been invented yet.

By the time the Wright brothers had grown up, the first cars were rumbling down the roads. Modern-looking bicycles were popular, too. And in 1903, Wilbur and Orville did something that made them both famous. They were the first inventors to build an airplane and fly it!

The two brothers grew up in and around Dayton, Ohio. Their father, Milton, was a minister who traveled from place to place. Sometimes the family had to move, too.

Wherever they lived, the boys found a place to set up a workshop. Their mother said that they loved to tinker, just the way she did. Susan Wright could fix almost anything. Sometimes she made toys for Wilbur and Orville and their big brothers and little sister.

Wilbur and Orville also made toys.
They made other things, too. Orville
liked to make kites. His friends saw that
his kite flew better than theirs. Soon,
Orville was selling kites to his friends.

One day, Orville invented a new kind
of gum. He mixed tar and sugar. But not
all inventions work. His friends did not
like the gum—it tasted awful!

Wilbur helped his father write a church newspaper. He ran the press that printed the newspaper. He also built a machine that folded the newspapers for mailing.

Orville became interested in printing, too. When he was 17 and Wilbur was 22, they went into business together. At first, they ran their own newspaper. Then they began printing newspapers, posters, and ads for other people in Dayton. One of their jobs was printing a newspaper for Orville's friend, Paul Laurence Dunbar. Later Paul Laurence Dunbar became famous as a poet.

When they were not working, both
brothers liked to ride bicycles. A new
kind of bike had just been invented. It
was called the safety bicycle. It had two
wheels that were of equal size. It had
brakes, too.

Wilbur liked to take long, quiet rides
on country lanes.

But Orville liked to go fast. He rode in races. He had fun, but he did not win any prizes.

When their bicycles broke, the Wright brothers were able to fix them. Soon, friends were coming by the printing shop with their broken bicycles.

Before long, Wilbur and Orville had a new business fixing broken bicycles. They sold and rented bicycles, too.

The Wright brothers were always busy. They fixed things around the house. They had their own camera and built themselves a darkroom to print their photographs.

Wilbur and Orville also spent lots of time reading. They read a lot about a man named Otto Lilienthal. He was called the "Flying Man." Otto Lilienthal had made almost 2,000 glides from hilltops. During these glides, he wore a huge pair of wings. But he could not balance the glider very well. The glider had no power of its own. It just rode on the wind.

He was only able to stay in the air for ten or fifteen seconds.

The Wright brothers read about Otto Lilienthal's gliders and the work of other inventors. Was it really possible to build a machine that could fly? Wilbur and Orville believed it was. So they set out to find a way to fly.

Wilbur and Orville wrote letters to find out more about flying. They got advice and more books to read. They decided that a safe flying machine would need to have three things:

1. wings to lift it into the air,
2. an engine to give it power, and
3. controls that would let the pilot balance the machine as it flew.

Then they began to test their ideas.
They built models. They built their own
glider. At first, they flew it like a kite.
It worked very well.

The brothers needed a big, open space to test their glider. They also wanted a place where there was lots of wind.

In 1900, they went to Kitty Hawk, North Carolina. They lived in a tent on the sand while they tested the glider. Sometimes the glider flew well. Other times it crashed. Wilbur and Orville fixed the glider many times.

At Kitty Hawk, the brothers made friends with Bill and Addie Tate and their family. Bill Tate sometimes helped them fly the glider.

When the brothers left Kitty Hawk, they gave the big glider to the Tates. Addie Tate took off the white cloth that covered the glider's wings. She used the cloth to make dresses for her two little girls.

Back in Ohio, Wilbur and Orville kept building bigger and better gliders. They tested each of their new designs. Soon, they were taking turns piloting a one-person glider.

Each day, they learned new things. "Wilbur and I could hardly wait for morning to come," Orville once said. "To get at something that interests us, that's happiness."

Finally, in 1903, they believed they had an airplane that would fly. In most ways, their plane looked like the gliders they had flown before. But this airplane was different because it had an engine and two propellers. They called it, *The Flyer*.

The brothers went back to Kitty Hawk.

All along, they had taken turns flying their gliders. Who would be the first to fly *The Flyer*? They solved the problem by flipping a coin.

Wilbur won the coin toss. He would be the first to fly *The Flyer*.

It was a very cold and windy December day. *The Flyer* rose into the air! Then Wilbur made a mistake at the controls. The plane crashed into the soft sand.

Wilbur was not hurt, but the brothers had to fix *The Flyer* before they could try again.

This time, Orville was the pilot. It was still very windy. Orville had a hard time balancing the plane in the air. But he kept the flying machine in the air for 12 seconds. After that, they flew again and again.

Their longest flight that day lasted 59 seconds.

When they got home, the brothers talked to the press. No big stories about their flight appeared in the newspapers because the reporters did not believe them! Scientists of the day did not believe people would ever be able to fly.

The Wright brothers kept working on planes. They made planes that had better controls. They made planes that were big enough for a passenger as well as a pilot.

By 1908, the Wright brothers were famous. That year, Wilbur flew an airplane in France. This time he stayed in the air for more than 90 minutes. More than 10,000 people watched and cheered Wilbur Wright's flight.

Today, airplanes travel across the country, around the world, and into space. Some planes, like the Concorde, can travel faster than the speed of sound. Powerful spaceships, like the shuttle *Discovery*, take astronauts into space.

The Wright brothers will always be remembered as the men who dreamed, and tinkered, and flew.

long a with final e long i with final e

airplane	advice
became	bike
brakes	decided
lanes	glides
made	glider
make	kite
mistake	like
named	prizes
place	ride
plane	size
races	sometimes
safe	time
safety	write
take	
taken	
tasted	
Tate	

believe   bicycle   business
famous   newspaper

controls   engine   machine
propellers   sugar

23